W9-AMV-980

THE BIG BOOK OF DINOSAURS

Dougal Dixon

THE BIG BOOK OF
DINOSAURS

An Hachette UK Company
www.hachette.co.uk

First published in the USA in 2013 by TickTock, an imprint of Octopus Publishing Group Ltd
Endeavour House
189 Shaftesbury Avenue
London, WC2H 8JY
www.octopusbooks.co.uk
www.octopusbooksusa.com

Distributed in the US by
Hachette Book Group USA
237 Park Avenue
New York NY 10017, USA

Distributed in Canada by
Canadian Manda Group
165 Dufferin Street
Toronto, Ontario, Canada M6K 3H6

ISBN 978 1 84898 746 3

Printed and bound in China
10 9 8 7 6 5 4 3 2 1

Picture credits (t=top; b=bottom; c=center; bg=background, l=left; r=right; OFC=outside front cover): American Museum of Natural History: 50–51. Photos 12/Alamy: 31bl. Leonello Calvetti and Luca Massini: 51br. Corbis: 16–17, 35br, 61cr, 66tr, 67cr, 69br. David & Sarah Cousens, AKA Cool Surface: 15b, 67br. FLPA: 77tl. Getty: 27tl. iStock: 19br, 28–29bg. Andrew Kerr: 6–7. Leonardo Meschini: 8–9, 10–11, 14, 22–23c, 23tl, tr, 24, 25, 34l, 42–43, 46t, 60–61c, 70br. Library of Congress/Science Photo Library: 22bl. NHM (London) De Agostini: 31bl. Rex Features/Everett Collection: 31tl, c. David Shepherd: 40–41, 62–63. Shutterstock: OFCbg, 2–3, 4–5, 12–13, 14–15bg, 18bl, 19bl, 20c, tr, 36–37bg, 21 (all), 22–23bg, 23 br, 24–25bg, 26cl, 31br, 36–37bg, 38cl, bl, 39tr, br, 40–41bg, 44tr, br, 46bl, 47c, br, 48t, 49t, 54–55, 57tl, br, 58–59, 60cl, 61br, tr, 62–63bg, 64–65, 66cl, 66–67bg, 68cl, 71(all), 72–73, 74–75, 77bc. TickTock archive: OFC, 18–19c, 19cr, 20l, 22t, 26bl, 26–27c, 29c, 32–33, 34tr, 35bl, tr, 36–37c, 38–39c, 44–45c, 45tr, 47tl, 48–49c, 49r, c, 52–53, 56–57c, 57tr, bl, 66–67bg, 68–69c, 69tr, 70tl, 73tr, 76, 77tr.

Every effort has been made to trace copyright holders, and we apologize in advance for any omissions.
We would be pleased to insert the appropriate acknowledgments in any subsequent edition of this publication.

CONTENTS

INTRODUCTION

We know much more about dinosaurs today than we did when they were first studied nearly 200 years ago. However, our knowledge is still incomplete and there is still so much to find out.

Scientists find out more by asking questions. They may pose a question about how a particular dinosaur gathered its food and then try to find the answer. They look at the evidence from the fossils themselves. Are the teeth a particular shape? Would the claws work better at slashing flesh than they would at ripping bark from trees? Often they look at modern animals and their lifestyles and compare them with what is known about dinosaurs. The sharp curved talons of an eagle are used for snatching small prey. If a small, meat-eating dinosaur had similar talons, does that mean it hunted similar prey? The hard shell of an armadillo is very effective at defending it from meat eaters. Does this mean that dinosaurs with hard shells were well protected from meat-eating dinosaurs?

The answers are not always easy to find. Sometimes there is very little evidence, so experts use a great deal of guesswork to come up with an answer. The next discovery may confirm whether the guess was right or wrong. Piece by piece, as the answers come together, we get a more accurate idea of what the dinosaurs were like and how they lived.

In this book, you will find the answers to all the dinosaur questions you have been dying to ask, as well as many more you would never have thought of asking. From essential facts about when and where dinosaurs lived, to the gory details of how dinosaur dung was fossilized, it's all you need to know about dinosaurs.

PREHISTORIC **TIMELINE**

Lagosuchus

Lystrosaurus

Lesothosaurus

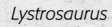

Mixosaurus

Eudimorphodon

Megalosaurus

Triassic—251 million to 199.6 million years ago
The period during which the dinosaurs first evolved.

Jurassic—199.6 million to 145.5 million years ago

Eoraptor

Coelophysis

Huayangosaurus

Dilophosaurus

Plateosaurus

Dimorphodon

Stegosaurus

Plesiosaurus

The dinosaurs' heyday, known as the Age of the Reptiles.

Diplodocus

Apatosaurus

Microraptor

Velociraptor

Iguanodon

Spinosaurus

Euoplocephalus

Saltasaurus

Cretaceous—145.5 million to 65.5 million years ago
The climax of dinosaur times, with more species evolving than ever.

Deinonychus

Bactrosaurus

Acrocanthosaurus

Muttaburrasaurus

Ankylosaurus

Triceratops

WHAT WAS A **DINOSAUR?**

A dinosaur was a land-living Mesozoic reptile. Find an animal with all these features, and you have a dinosaur.

1. Limbs for walking held vertically beneath the body.

2. A flange on the upper arm holding powerful muscles.

3. Three or more vertebrae attached to the hip bones. Three or fewer bones in the fourth finger. Most meat-eating dinosaurs had only three fingers and had no bones in the fourth.

4. A hole, rather than a socket, in the hip for holding the femur, or thighbone.

5. A ball-like top to the femur, to fit the hole in the hip.

6. A strong joint between the foot bones and the bones of the hind leg.

7. A specific number and arrangement of bones in the skull.

③

①

WHERE DID DINOSAURS **LIVE?**

ALASKA
Early Cretaceous fossils

EASTERN GREENLAND
Late Triassic fossils

Middle Jurassic

*Triassic,
Jurassic,
Cretaceous*

Late Triassic

*Cretaceous
Middle Jurassic*

*Cretaceous
Late Jurassic*

MEXICO
Middle Jurassic fossils

Early Cretaceous

MALI
Late Cretaceous fossils

VENEZUELA
Early Jurassic fossils

Earth was a very different place when
the dinosaurs were alive. The landmasses
that have evolved into the continents
of today were a completely different shape.
This map shows where the principal
dinosaur fossil finds have been made
around the world in recent decades.

Increasing number of
dinosaur sites 1992–2004

- Late Triassic
- Early Jurassic
- Middle Jurassic
- Late Jurassic
- Early Cretaceous
- Late Cretaceous

- ○ Established areas
- ♈ Tracks
- ◉ Fossils

Late Cretaceous

ANTARCTIC PENINSULA
Late Cretaceous fossils

ANTARCTICA, TRANSANTARCTIC MOUNTAINS
Middle Jurassic fossils

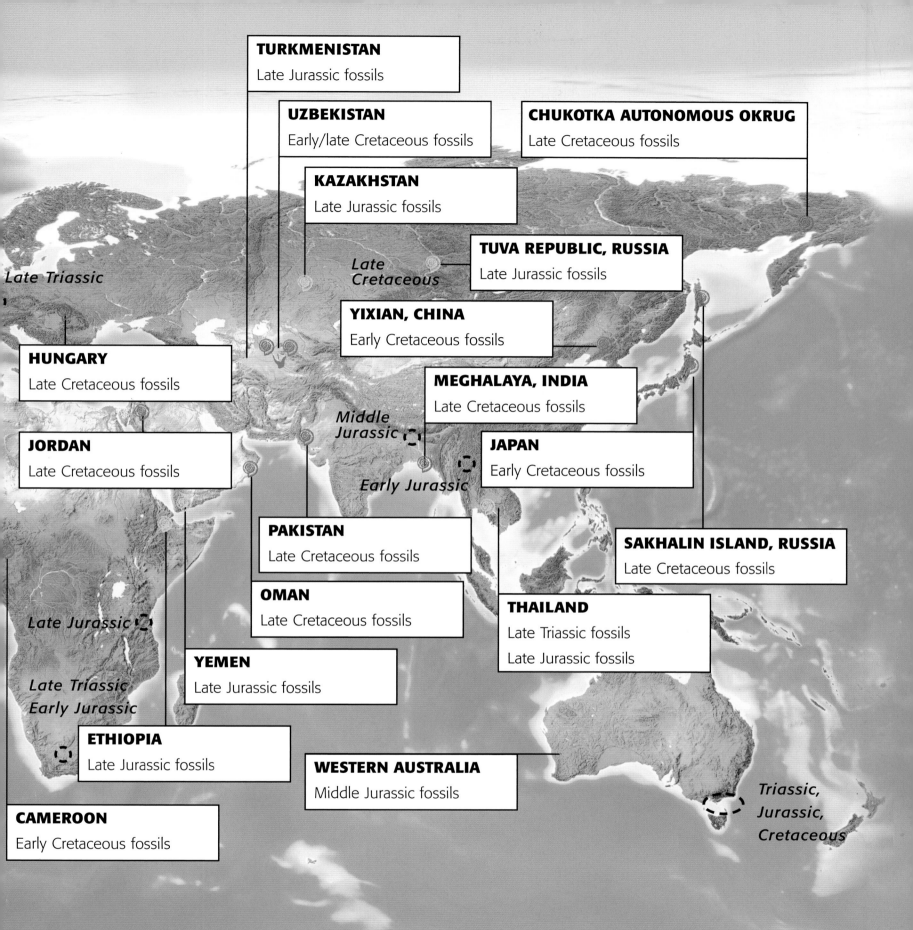

TURKMENISTAN
Late Jurassic fossils

UZBEKISTAN
Early/late Cretaceous fossils

CHUKOTKA AUTONOMOUS OKRUG
Late Cretaceous fossils

KAZAKHSTAN
Late Jurassic fossils

Late Cretaceous

TUVA REPUBLIC, RUSSIA
Late Jurassic fossils

Late Triassic

YIXIAN, CHINA
Early Cretaceous fossils

HUNGARY
Late Cretaceous fossils

MEGHALAYA, INDIA
Late Cretaceous fossils

Middle Jurassic

JORDAN
Late Cretaceous fossils

JAPAN
Early Cretaceous fossils

Early Jurassic

PAKISTAN
Late Cretaceous fossils

SAKHALIN ISLAND, RUSSIA
Late Cretaceous fossils

OMAN
Late Cretaceous fossils

THAILAND
Late Triassic fossils
Late Jurassic fossils

Late Jurassic

YEMEN
Late Jurassic fossils

Late Triassic
Early Jurassic

ETHIOPIA
Late Jurassic fossils

WESTERN AUSTRALIA
Middle Jurassic fossils

Triassic, Jurassic, Cretaceous

CAMEROON
Early Cretaceous fossils

MYTH VS. FACT

Did dinosaurs have feathers?

China

The meat-eating dinosaurs are closely related to modern birds. Some of the smaller ones were even covered in feathers. Many people found this difficult to believe, until many fossilized dinosaurs, birds, and half-dinosaur-half-birds were found in China in the 1990s. Some of these fossils were preserved in such detail that they even show the feathers.

Was it only the meat eaters that had feathers?

Most people thought so, but in 2009, a fossil of a plant-eating dinosaur with feathers turned up in China. Measuring only around 27 in. (70 cm) long and related to the larger *Heterodontosaurus*, this early Cretaceous creature (shown right) was given the name *Tianyulong*.

Does a dinosaur skeleton always show the animal's size when it was alive?

We used to think so. Then an exceptionally well-preserved hadrosaur, or duck-billed dinosaur, was discovered in North Dakota in 1999. The vertebrae were separated by gaps that, in life, would have been filled with lots of gristle. This would have made the total length of the animal around 15 percent greater than if it had been measured by the bones alone.

Did boneheaded dinosaurs butt their heads together like mountain goats?

There are lots of dramatic pictures of big, angry boneheaded dinosaurs such as *Pachycephalosaurus* butting their heads together. However, recent discoveries and studies show that the domes were the wrong shape—they would have just bounced off one another. It is more likely that these dinosaurs used their heads as battering rams, to bash into the flanks of an enemy.

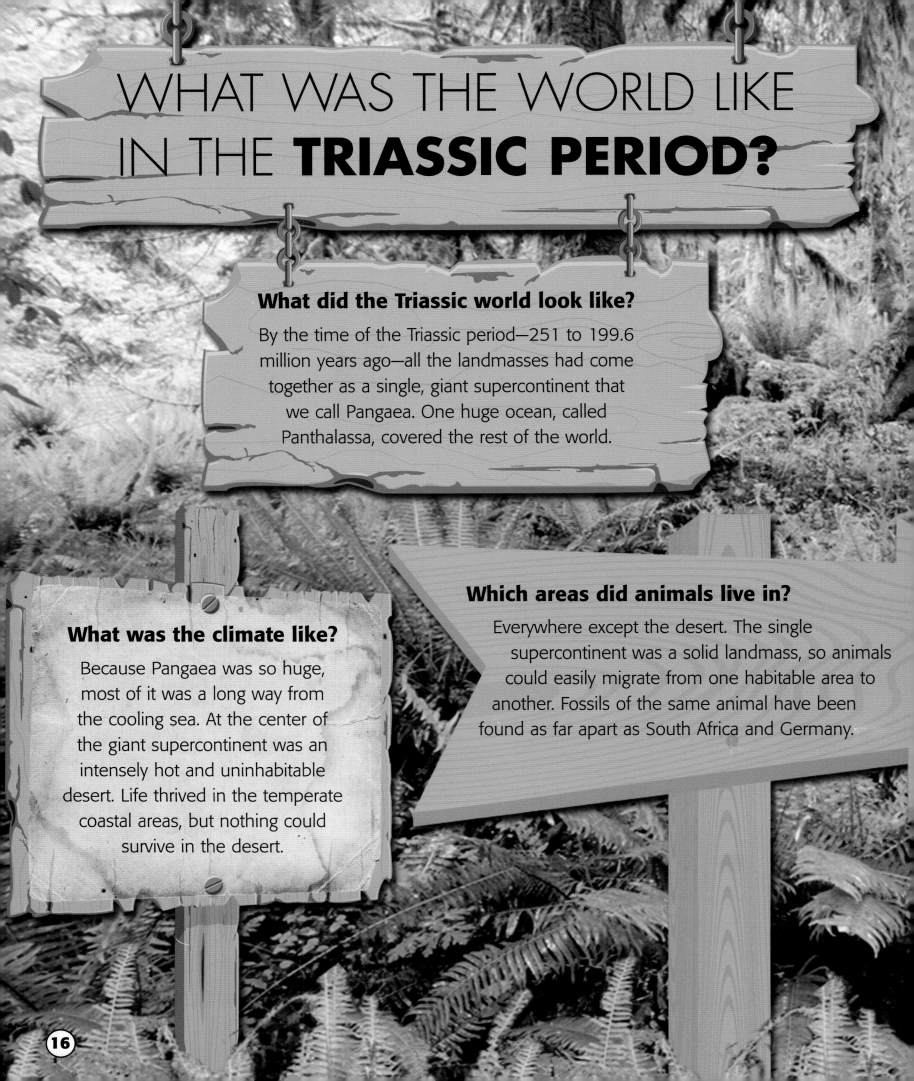

WHAT WAS THE WORLD LIKE IN THE **TRIASSIC PERIOD?**

What did the Triassic world look like?

By the time of the Triassic period—251 to 199.6 million years ago—all the landmasses had come together as a single, giant supercontinent that we call Pangaea. One huge ocean, called Panthalassa, covered the rest of the world.

What was the climate like?

Because Pangaea was so huge, most of it was a long way from the cooling sea. At the center of the giant supercontinent was an intensely hot and uninhabitable desert. Life thrived in the temperate coastal areas, but nothing could survive in the desert.

Which areas did animals live in?

Everywhere except the desert. The single supercontinent was a solid landmass, so animals could easily migrate from one habitable area to another. Fossils of the same animal have been found as far apart as South Africa and Germany.

Were there icecaps?

There is no geological evidence of ice in the Triassic period, unlike the earlier Permian period, which had an ice age.

How long was a day?

The Triassic day was probably only around 23 hours long because the world was spinning a little faster then.

Where does the word *Triassic* come from?

It literally means "threefold." Geologists working in Germany in 1834 noticed three types of rocks from this time and named the Triassic period after the discovery.

Was there vegetation?

In the forest, there were tree ferns, conifers, and horsetails.

TYRANNOSAURUS

What type of animal was *Tyrannosaurus*?

Tyrannosaurus, and its relatives among the tyrannosaurs, belonged to the meat-eating group of dinosaurs. We call these theropods, or "beast-footed."

Its eyes pointing forward, to focus on *its kill*

Did *Tyrannosaurus*

 ROAR?

Only in movies! Judging by the volume of the neck and throat, as well as how the skull bones resonated, *Tyrannosaurus* probably made more of a croak like a bullfrog.

It had poisonous saliva, from rotting flesh stuck between the teeth

bullfrog   **CROAK**

Did *Tyrannosaurus* only have two clawed fingers?

It did have traces of a third, but it was so small that it would have been invisible in the flesh of the hand.

How much did a *Tyrannosaurus* weigh?

Until 2009, 4.5 metric tons was the figure given for the weight of *Tyrannosaurus*. However, new research suggests that the weights of all dinosaurs had been overestimated because of a mathematical flaw. The revised weight is around 3 metric tons.

Tyrannosaurus was 42 ft. (12.8 m) long

How quickly did *Tyrannosaurus* grow?

A young *Tyrannosaurus* grew very quickly, reaching maturity at around the age of 14. After that, it did not grow much at all.

How many types of teeth did *Tyrannosaurus* have?

The teeth at the side were 6 in. (15 cm) long, thin, and bladelike, with steak-knife serrations on the front and rear edges. These were for slicing through meat. Those at the front were shorter, thicker, and stronger. These were for holding on to struggling prey.

Did *Tyrannosaurus* have a strong bite?

All meat-eating dinosaurs had a joint halfway along the lower jaw. This gave the jaw freedom of movement to help in eating and gathering food. In *Tyrannosaurus,* this joint was solid and immovable. Its bite was strong enough to tear through tough flesh and crush thick bones.

DID YOU **KNOW . . . ?**

Could meat eaters kill with a bite?

Pieces of flesh may have stuck between dinosaurs' teeth and become infected, resulting in a bite that could weaken or kill prey.

How do we know what *Tyrannosaurus* ate?

We know that it ate other dinosaurs because a *Triceratops* skeleton was found with around 80 toothmarks and wounds along the backbone and huge bone-scraping eating wounds all along the hip bones.

What happened if a dinosaur broke a tooth?

Dinosaurs' teeth grew throughout their lifetime, so if one broke, it would be replaced. It is the same today with crocodiles!

Dino droppings

Fossilized dung (coprolite) can also reveal what dinosaurs ate. For example, *Tyrannosaurus* dung (17 in./44 cm long and with a volume of 0.62 gal./2.4 L) has been found containing bone fragments from a duck-billed dinosaur.

Which was the heaviest dinosaur?

The heaviest dinosaur is believed to be the *Brachiosaurus*. It weighed 80 metric tons—the weight of *17 African elephants!*

How did *Allosaurus* kill its prey?

The strength of the skull, the wide hinging of the lower jaw, and the muscles of the neck suggest that it could bring its great open mouth down like a massive hammer on the back of its poor victim, killing it instantly.

Did dinosaurs have two brains?

In the past, there was a theory that some of the large dinosaurs, for example, *Brachiosaurus* and *Stegosaurus*, had a second brain. Paleontologists now realize that this was an enlargement in the spinal cord in the hip area.

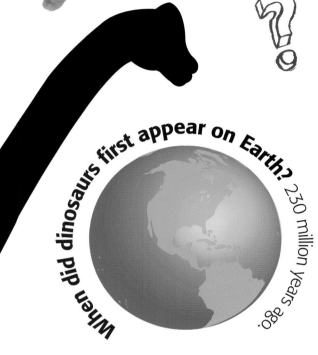

When did dinosaurs first appear on Earth? 230 million years ago.

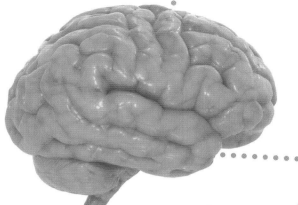

What is the biggest egg?

The largest dinosaur egg is 18 in. (45 cm) long and 6 in. (15 cm) in diameter—that's bigger than a soccer ball! It was laid by a huge tyrannosaur and was found in China in the 1970s.

What is the smallest dinosaur egg?

The smallest dinosaur eggs come from Thailand and are the size of the eggs of a European robin.

Did any dinosaur eat the eggs of others?

They must have. Eggs are too good a source of protein to miss. We used to think that *Oviraptor* was an egg stealer (that is what the name means). Now we are not so sure, but it is difficult to see what else the strong jaws and the teeth at the top of the mouth could have been used for.

DINOSAUR **NAMES**

Why do we sometimes call everyone's favorite dinosaur "T. rex"?

It is a short way of saying it. The full name is *Tyrannosaurus rex—Tyrannosaurus* is the genus name and *rex* is the species name. All dinosaurs (in fact, all living things) have two-part names like this—yours as a human being is *Homo sapiens*.

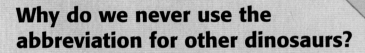

Why do we never use the abbreviation for other dinosaurs?

We should, if we want to be consistent. For example, there are several species of *Diplodocus* that we could abbreviate, but that would imply that we can tell the difference between them—which we cannot!

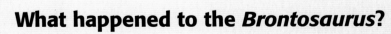

What happened to the *Brontosaurus*?

We now call it *Apatosaurus*. *Brontosaurus* was discovered in 1879 by Othniel Charles Marsh (left). Years later, it was revealed that the remains Marsh had found in 1877 and named *Apatosaurus* were actually from the same animal. The rules state that the first name given is the one that sticks, so from 1974, *Apatosaurus* was used instead of *Brontosaurus*.

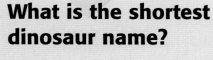

What is the longest dinosaur name?

Micropachycephalosaurus

The name means "tiny, thick-headed lizard" and has a total of 23 letters.

What is the shortest dinosaur name?

Mei, meaning "soundly sleeping." Its full name is *Mei long*, "soundly sleeping dragon" in Chinese.

How do we say "dinosaur" in . . .

French?
dinosaure

Hungarian?
dinoszarurusz

German?
dinosaurier

Japanese?
kyouryuu

Spanish?
dinosaurio

Italian?
dinosauro

How do we name dinosaurs?

They are usually named after the place where they were found, a feature of their appearance, or a famous person. For example, *Crichtonsaurus* was named after Michael Crichton, the author of the book *Jurassic Park*.

DINOSAUR **FAMILIES**

How did a baby dinosaur differ from an adult?

As is the case with most animals, baby dinosaurs had a bigger head and bigger feet than adults in relation to their body size. Hatchlings of the prosauropod *Massospondylus* crawled on all fours before becoming two-footed adults— possibly because of the size of their heads.

Was the atmosphere different from today?

There was probably more oxygen and carbon dioxide, encouraging both animal life and plant growth. Insects thrived, and the first bird, *Archaeopteryx*, appeared.

How had the climate changed?

The opening of the continents formed a seaway all the way around the world in the region of the equator. Constant westward-flowing currents along this seaway led to milder and moister climates.

DINOSAURS AT THE MOVIES

When did dinosaurs first appear on the movie screen?

In 1912, a series of short movies was produced featuring a cartoon sauropod named Gertie.

What was the first dinosaur feature-length movie?

The first big movie was *The Lost World* (1925), based on the book by Sir Arthur Conan Doyle. It is about a group of explorers who find dinosaurs living in South America.

What was the first full-length dinosaur cartoon?

Dinosaurs featured in Walt Disney's *Fantasia* in 1940.

What is the most famous dinosaur movie of recent years?

It is *Jurassic Park* (1993), based on the novel by Michael Crichton and directed by Steven Spielberg.

Why was the movie title *Jurassic Park* incorrect?

Because almost all the dinosaurs featured actually came from the next period, the Cretaceous!

How do they recreate dinosaurs in movies?

They used to do it by stop-motion animation. A model dinosaur was moved a little bit at a time, and one frame of film was taken for each movement, as in *King Kong* (1933).

Sometimes they used a man in a dinosaur costume, as in *The Last Dinosaur* (1967). They also used to stick fins and horns onto lizards and film them in slow motion, as in *Journey to the Center of the Earth* (1958).

Nowadays, they tend to use computer-generated imagery, as in Disney's *Dinosaur* (2000), which combined live-action backgrounds and animated dinosaurs, and the remake of *King Kong* (2005). As shown below, this last movie features a *Tyrannosaurus* battling with King Kong.

COULD DINOSAURS **FLY?**

No. Some very small, feathered dinosaurs such as *Microraptor* glided from tree to tree but would not have actually flown. When people talk about "flying dinosaurs," they are usually referring to the pterosaurs—creatures that were closely related to dinosaurs but not actually dinosaurs themselves.

DID YOU **KNOW . . . ?**

How many fingers did dinosaurs have?

Plant-eating ornithopods usually had five. Duck-billed dinosaurs had three fingers that sometimes fused together in a fleshy mitt to take the animal's weight while it was walking. Meat eaters had three fingers, or sometimes two, as in the case of the later tyrannosaurs. One group, the alvarezsaurids (shown right), only had a single finger with a huge claw on the forelimb.

What is a chimera?

In Greek mythology, a chimera was a monster with two heads—one of a lion and one of a goat—and a tail in the form of a snake. Paleontologists use the term to describe a skeleton that has been mistakenly built from the remains of more than one type of animal. For example, a sauropod described in 1979 and called *Ultrasauros* actually turned out to be parts of a *Brachiosaurus* combined with parts of a *Supersaurus*. Nobody knows how the parts got mixed up!

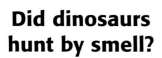

Did dinosaurs hunt by smell?

We do not know for sure, but probably not. It is really only mammals that hunt by smell.

Why does horn never fossilize?

Horn is made of the substance keratin, found in fingernails. Although hard, keratin rots very quickly. Also, many insects like to eat horn, so it never has a chance to fossilize.

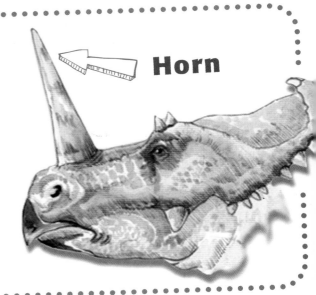

Horn

Did any dinosaurs have fangs?

Heterodontosaurus, a small ornithopod, had a beak at the front of the mouth, a pair of fang-shaped, doglike teeth at the side, and plant-chopping teeth at the back. Its name means "lizard with all types of teeth"!

How long does the excavation of a dinosaur take?

The longest dinosaur excavation on record was around 100 years. Builders digging foundations for a bridge in Connecticut in the 1880s found the rear half of a skeleton of the prosauropod *Ammosaurus*. The front half was actually built into the bridge and was not completely recovered by paleontologists until the bridge was demolished in 1969.

HOW FAST COULD
DINOSAURS RUN?

It is very difficult to tell how quickly a dinosaur could run. The only evidence is from fossilized footprints, which can be very misleading. For example, the distance between the individual footprints can suggest how quickly the legs could move, but that depends on the length of the legs. Taking such factors into consideration, the best guess for the fastest dinosaur, a small meat eater such as *Gallimimus* (shown below), would be around 39 ft. (12 m) per second. That is about the same speed as an Olympic sprinter.

STEGOSAURUS

What type of animal was *Stegosaurus*?

Stegosaurus was a member of the group that we call the thyreophorans. These were all four-legged plant eaters and were either covered in armor (*Ankylosaurus*) or carried plates and spines (*Stegosaurus*).

How big was its brain?

Stegosaurus had one of the smallest brains of any dinosaur—only around the size of a walnut in a head the size of a horse.

Why do we think that *Stegosaurus* had cheeks?

There is a space for cheeks between the teeth and the outside of the skull. The teeth would therefore only work well with the food held in cheeks. However, some scientists think that, instead of cheeks, *Stegosaurus* had a beak. The surface of the jawbone is similar to the surface of a turtle's jawbone—and a turtle has a beak that runs along the length of the mouth.

How was the delicate neck protected?

A mass of little bony studs protected the throat like a covering of chain mail.

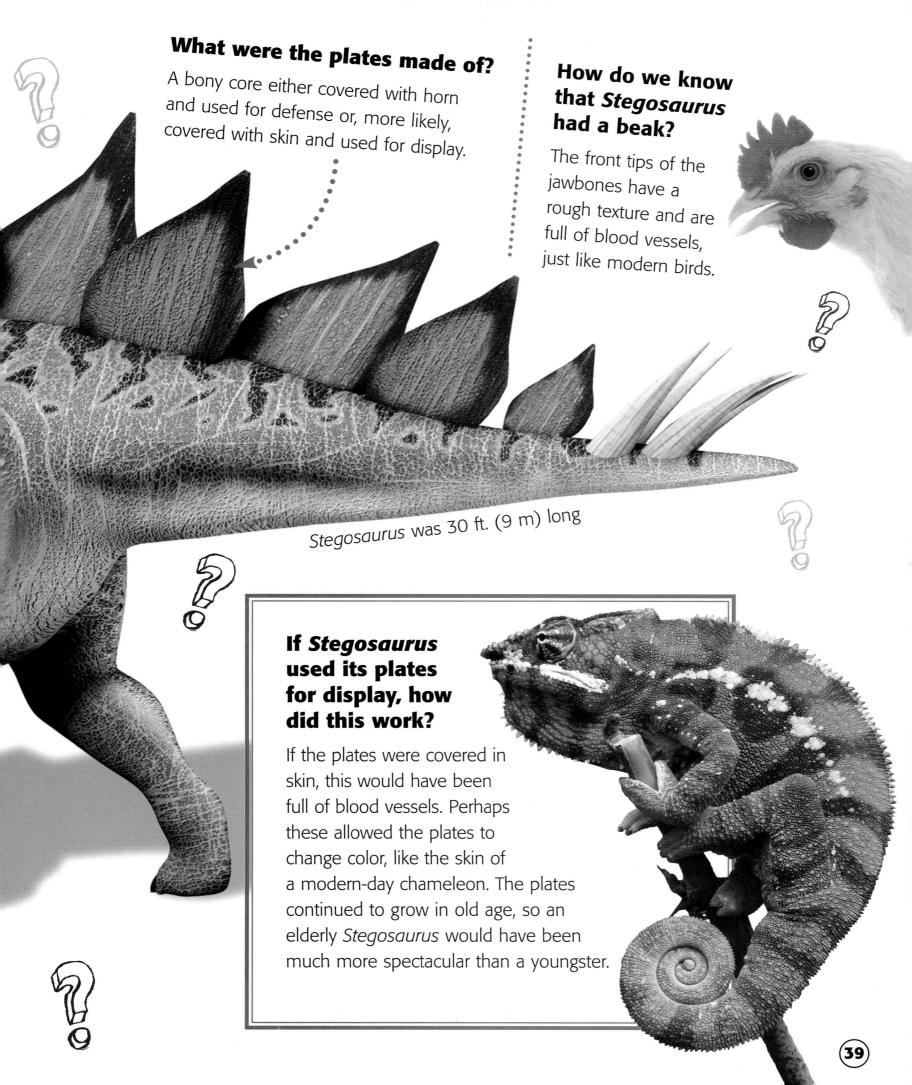

What were the plates made of?

A bony core either covered with horn and used for defense or, more likely, covered with skin and used for display.

How do we know that *Stegosaurus* had a beak?

The front tips of the jawbones have a rough texture and are full of blood vessels, just like modern birds.

Stegosaurus was 30 ft. (9 m) long

If *Stegosaurus* used its plates for display, how did this work?

If the plates were covered in skin, this would have been full of blood vessels. Perhaps these allowed the plates to change color, like the skin of a modern-day chameleon. The plates continued to grow in old age, so an elderly *Stegosaurus* would have been much more spectacular than a youngster.

19TH-CENTURY
DINOSAUR DISCOVERIES

The 1800s saw great scientific developments in the study of dinosaur remains. Because of this, a picture of dinosaurs as a group of actual living animals emerged.

Pachypodes!

1832
German paleontologist Hermann von Meyer names the animals found by Buckland and Mantell "pachypodes." The classification is not used.

1825
Gideon Mantell names *Iguanodon*.

1824
William Buckland names *Megalosaurus*.

1877-1897
American paleontologists Othniel Charles Marsh and Edward Drinker Cope compete to discover new dinosaurs. Known as the "Bone Wars," around 160 new dinosaurs are found by the end of the century.

1878
The discovery of a herd of *Iguanodon* in a mine in Belgium gives the first clear idea of what a whole dinosaur looked like.

1898
Barnum Brown finds the first *Tyrannosaurus* remains.

1833

The first armored dinosaur ever to be found is named *Hylaeosaurus* by Mantell.

1837

Von Meyer finds the first prosauropod, *Plateosaurus*.

Dinosauria!

1842

Sir Richard Owen comes up with the name "Dinosauria" to describe the animals known at this time. Unlike Meyer's suggestion, the name proves popular.

1858

American anatomist Joseph Leidy finds the duck-billed dinosaur *Hadrosaurus*.

1859

Charles Darwin publishes *On the Origin of Species*.

1853

The first dinosaur theme park opens in London, England, in the grounds of the Crystal Palace.

1855

The first dinosaurs are found in North America.

North America

WHAT WAS THE TAIL OF A **DIPLODOCUS** USED FOR?

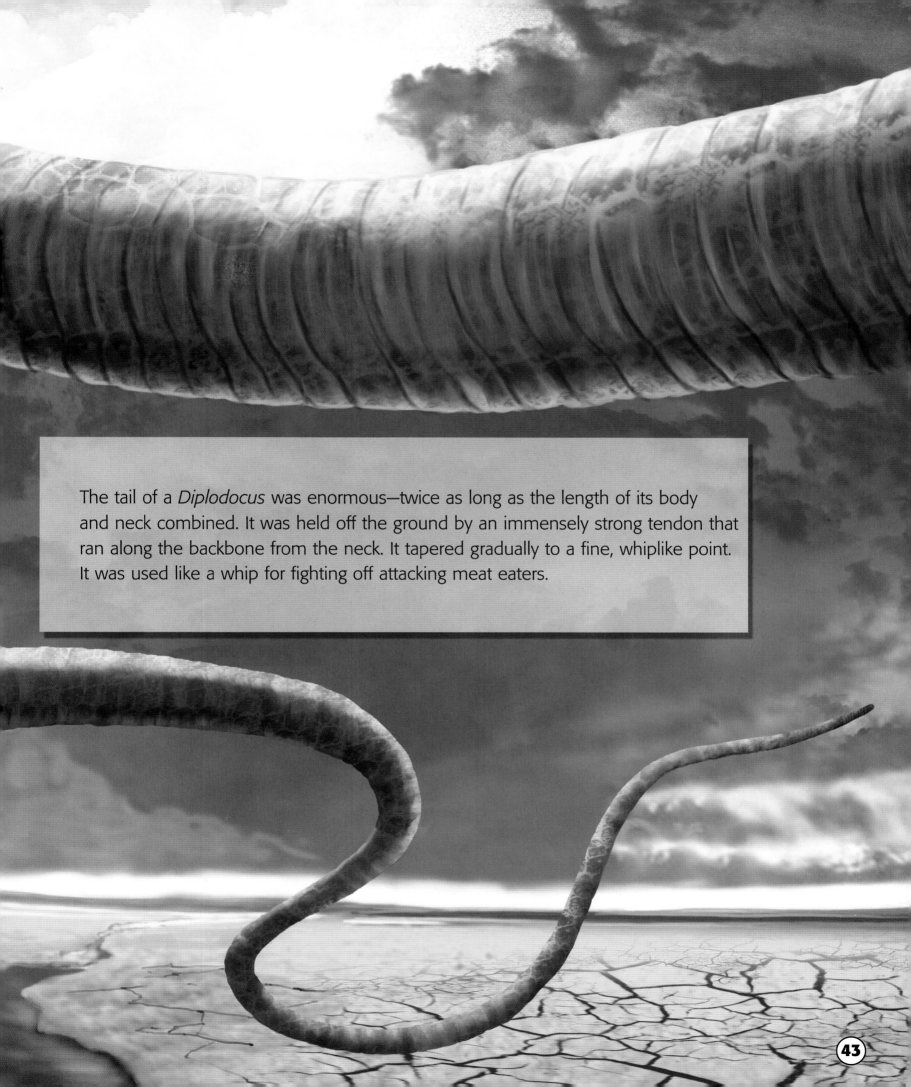

The tail of a *Diplodocus* was enormous—twice as long as the length of its body and neck combined. It was held off the ground by an immensely strong tendon that ran along the backbone from the neck. It tapered gradually to a fine, whiplike point. It was used like a whip for fighting off attacking meat eaters.

ANKYLOSAURUS

What type of animal was *Ankylosaurus*?

Ankylosaurus was the best-known member of the ankylosaur group. They were all four-legged plant eaters and covered in armor. They also had mighty tail clubs of bone and muscle that were highly effective weapons.

A knight's mace

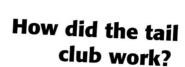

How did the tail club work?

The bones of the tail were bound together with tough tendons to make it stiff and straight, like the shaft of a medieval knight's mace. Using the muscle, the weapon could be swung from side to side with great power.

Was the club used for anything else?

Some scientists think that it may have had an eye-spot pattern that would make the club look like a head. Attacking meat eaters would take a bite and get a mouthful of bone!

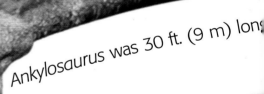

Ankylosaurus was 30 ft. (9 m) long

Are tails still used as weapons?

Yes, cows flick their tails angrily at irritating flies.

Did all ankylosaurs have tail clubs?

Sauropelta was a relative of *Ankylosaurus*, but instead of having a bony club on its tail, its defenses were on the neck and shoulders. Huge spikes pointed sideways and upward, protecting it from attacks from the front.

Armor covered its back

How much did it weigh?

Around 6 metric tons.

Its eyelids acted as armored shutters

Do modern animals have armor?

Some modern animals, such as the armadillo, have thick, scaly armor covering their bodies. It may not be as tough as a dinosaur's, but it does the same job!

Armadillo

45

DID YOU **KNOW . . .?**

How many boneheaded dinosaurs were there?

We are not really sure. *Dracorex* had no dome on its head, but it did have long spines, while *Stygimoloch* had a small dome with long spines around the back. The most famous of the boneheads is *Pachycephalosaurus,* which had a heavy dome on the top of the skull and knobs around the back of the head. However, some scientists believe that all three were the same animal, just at different stages of life.

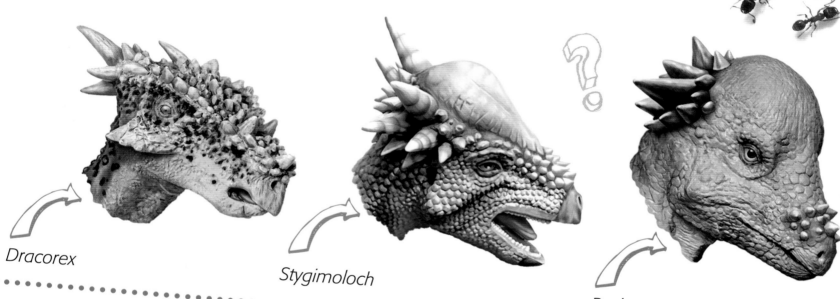

Dracorex

Stygimoloch

Pachycephalosaurus

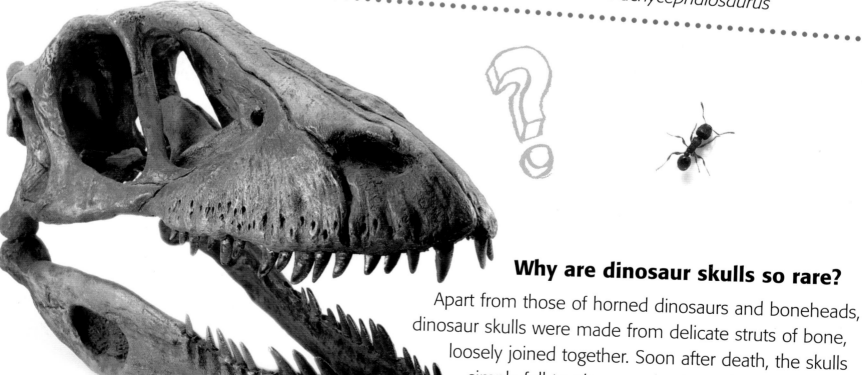

Why are dinosaur skulls so rare?

Apart from those of horned dinosaurs and boneheads, dinosaur skulls were made from delicate struts of bone, loosely joined together. Soon after death, the skulls simply fell to pieces and scattered.

Can you tell the sex of a *Tyrannosaurus*?

A male *Tyrannosaurus* had an extra bone at the base of its tail, which was part of its reproductive system.

Were there any anteater dinosaurs?

The alvarezsaurids, such as *Mononykus*, may have eaten ants. They had a single great claw on their hand, which they might have used to break into nests, and a long tongue to lap up the ants.

Did dinosaurs talk to one another?

The duck-billed dinosaur *Parasaurolophus* had a big, hollow crest connected to its nose passages. This allowed it to make a noise like a trombone to signal to the rest of the herd.

How are fossil sites protected?

Amateur collectors and professional thieves sometimes raid fossil sites. The best way to protect a fossil site is to cover it with a shelter and limit access to it.

WHAT COLOR
WERE DINOSAURS?

No one knows what color the dinosaurs were. Fossils do not reveal skin color. However, recent discoveries suggest that some were brightly colored. We know that they had good eyesight, and so body color would have been important to them.

What color were meat eaters?

They may have been striped and spotted like today's tigers and leopards. If so, this camouflage would have been useful when they were hunting.

Can we tell the color of feathered dinosaurs?

Early in 2010, scientists revealed that the theropod *Sinosauropteryx* from China would have been a reddish color with a striped tail. They figured this out by studying the microscopic structures that give bird feathers their color.

What color were the sauropods?

Big animals today—such as elephants and rhinos—are drab grays and browns. Maybe the biggest of the dinosaurs were similarly colored—but only MAYBE!

What color were ornithopods?

These dinosaurs may have been camouflaged with greens and browns to hide from the meat eaters.

ARE DINOSAUR FIGHTS EVER **PRESERVED?**

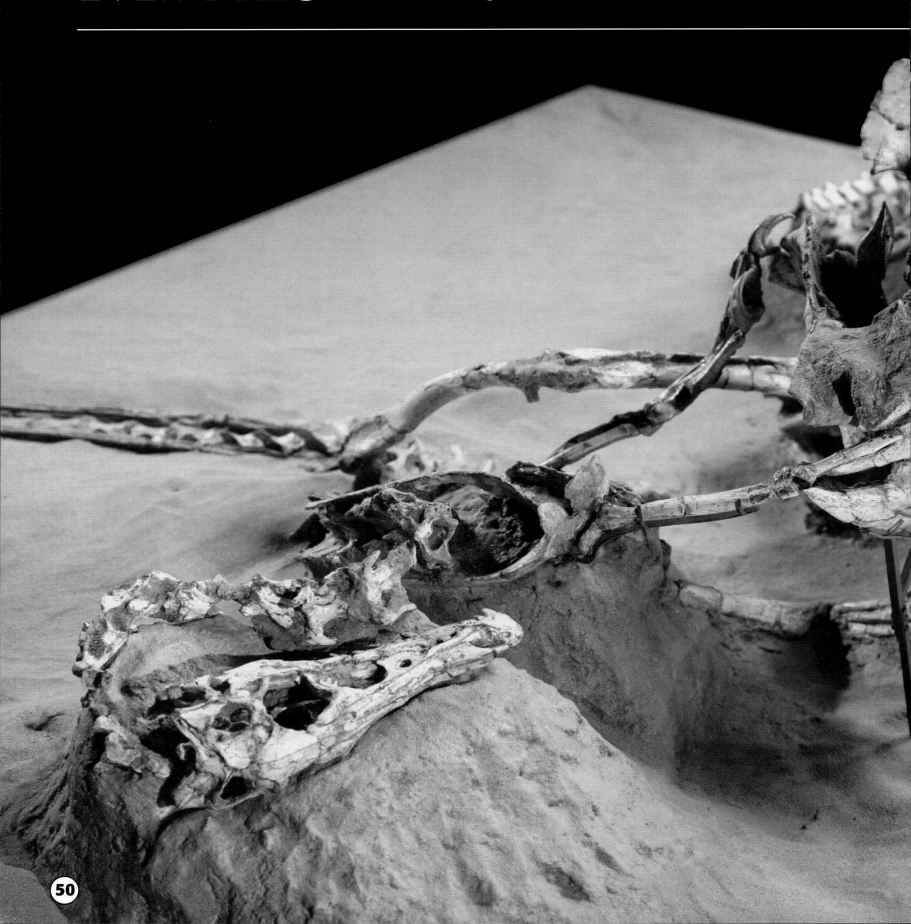

Yes. An expedition to Mongolia in 1971 uncovered the skeleton of a *Velociraptor* wound around that of a small ceratopsian, *Protoceratops* (shown below). They had been fighting when they were buried in a sandstorm.

A *Velociraptor* (left) fights with a *Protoceratops.*

DID DINOSAURS **HUNT IN PACKS?**

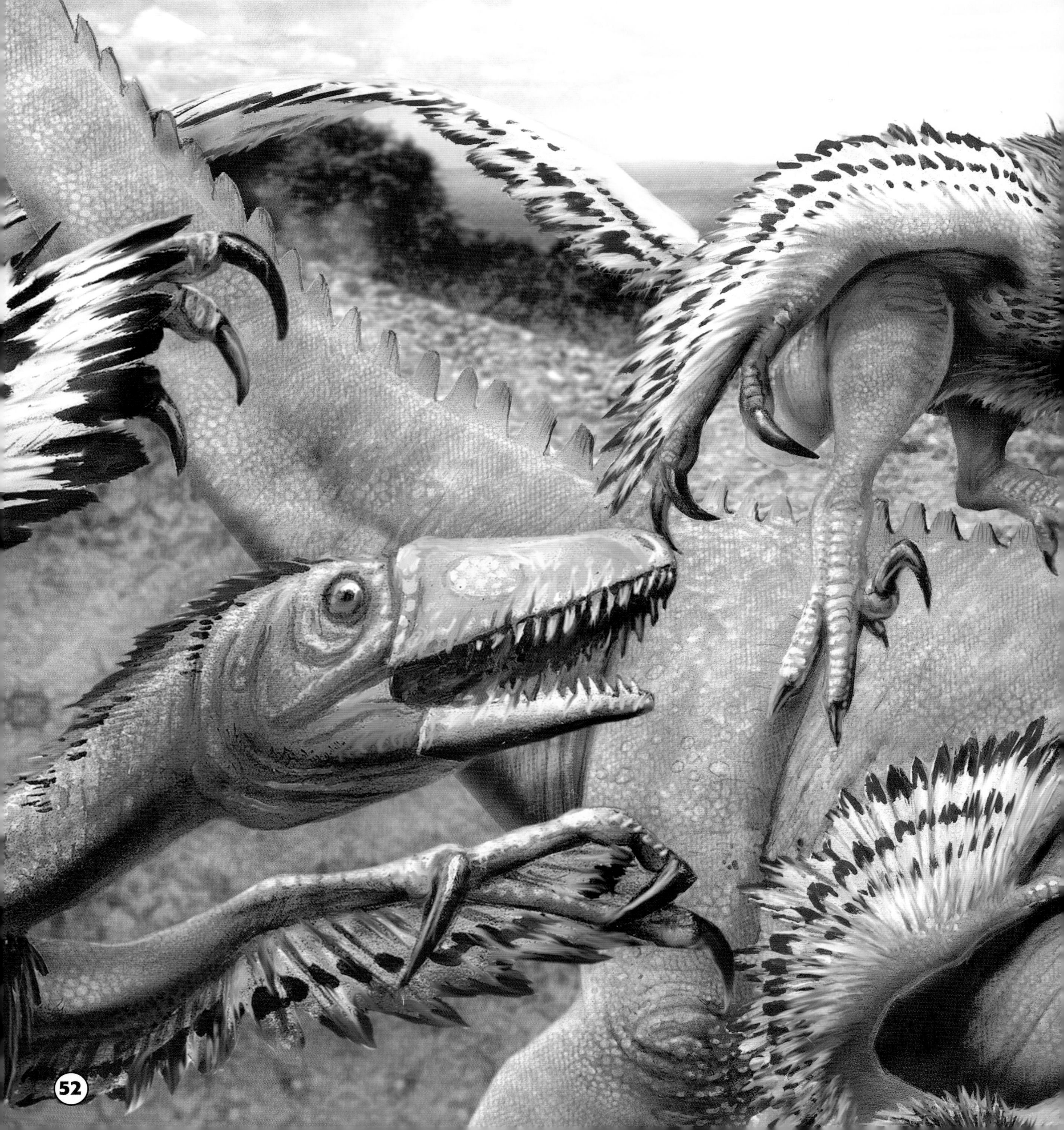

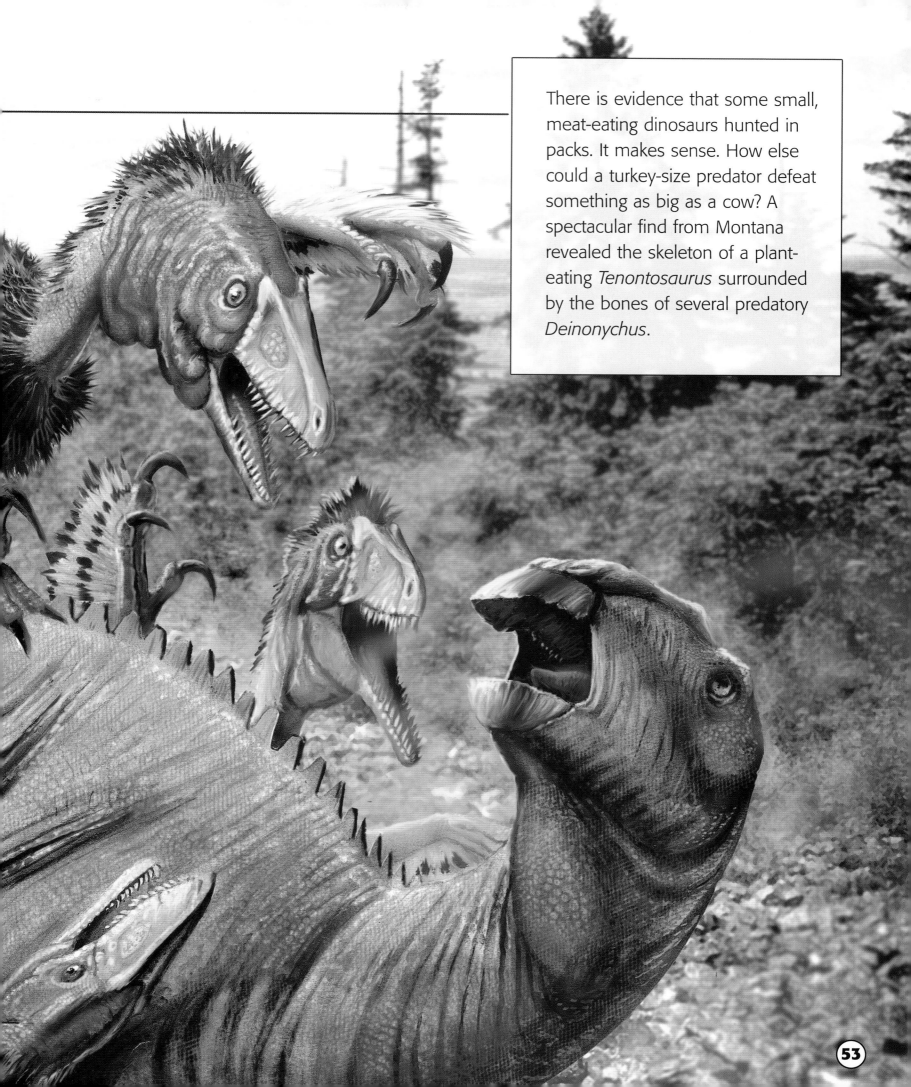

There is evidence that some small, meat-eating dinosaurs hunted in packs. It makes sense. How else could a turkey-size predator defeat something as big as a cow? A spectacular find from Montana revealed the skeleton of a plant-eating *Tenontosaurus* surrounded by the bones of several predatory *Deinonychus*.

DINOSAUR
BONES

How can we tell if a small skeleton was from a small dinosaur or just a large dinosaur baby?

Baby animals usually had bigger eyes, heads, and feet than adults in relation to their body size. Also, scientists can tell if the bones were fully formed and knitted together or not, as all this changed as the animal grew.

Why do skeletons sometimes show dinosaurs walking on their tiptoes?

Many dinosaurs, such as this *Tyrannosaurus*, really did walk on tiptoes. The bones of the foot were incorporated into the structure of the leg to make the leg longer and more agile.

Why, in a complete dinosaur fossil, is the head often thrown back and the tail dragged upward?

Scientists used to think that this was because the tendons that held the bones together dried out and shrank after the animal had died. Now, however, they think that this is due to the dinosaur thrashing around in pain before its death.

Why do we sometimes see two fossils that are mirror images of each other?

When a small dinosaur is fossilized, it is compressed and the remains lie flat between two beds of rock. When the rock is split open, half of the fossil is stuck to one slab, and the other half to the other. This is known as the "part and counterpart."

TRICERATOPS

What type of dinosaur was *Triceratops*?

Triceratops was the biggest of the group that we call the ceratopsians—the horned dinosaurs. The largest of these were four-legged plant eaters with horns. The smaller forms were two-legged.

When was *Triceratops* alive?

Triceratops was one of the last dinosaurs and lived at the very end of the Cretaceous period.

How were the horns arranged?

Two long ones pointed forward over the eyes and a short one above the nose.

What was the frill used for?

It probably evolved among the early ceratopsians as a ridge to hold the neck muscles. Then it became a shield to protect the neck and was probably brightly colored to act as a signal flag to other dinosaurs.

How much did it weigh?

A *Triceratops* weighed around 8 metric tons, the same weight as an empty truck!

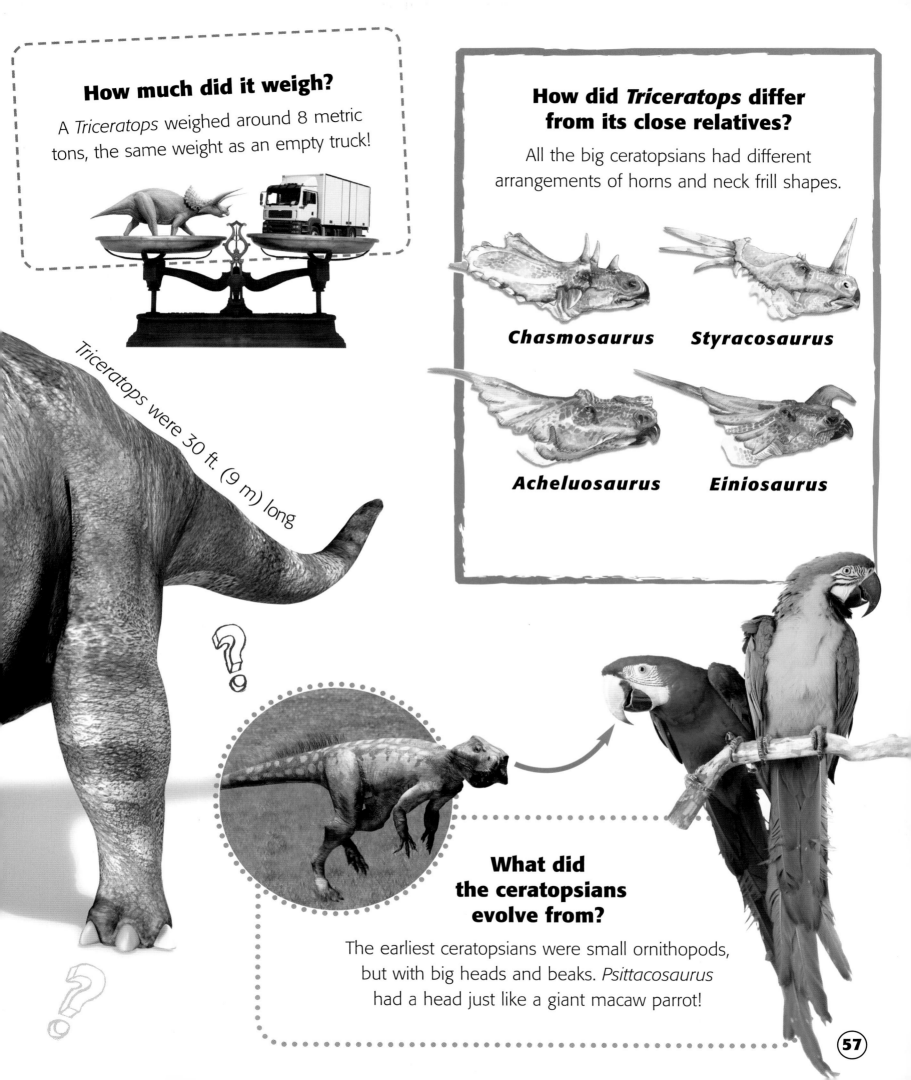

Triceratops were 30 ft. (9 m) long

How did *Triceratops* differ from its close relatives?

All the big ceratopsians had different arrangements of horns and neck frill shapes.

Chasmosaurus

Styracosaurus

Acheluosaurus

Einiosaurus

What did the ceratopsians evolve from?

The earliest ceratopsians were small ornithopods, but with big heads and beaks. *Psittacosaurus* had a head just like a giant macaw parrot!

WHAT WAS THE WORLD LIKE IN THE **CRETACEOUS PERIOD?**

1909
The great dinosaur deposits of Canada begin to be uncovered.

1907–1910
Eberhard Fraas of Stuttgart Museum collects dinosaurs in Tanzania (then German East Africa), including that of *Brachiosaurus*—the biggest mounted skeleton in the world.

1923
Roy Chapman Andrews of the American Museum of Natural History finds the first dinosaur nests and eggs, in Mongolia.

1951
Chinese expedition uncovers the big dinosaur deposits in central China.

1980
Luis and Walter Alvarez propose the theory of the asteroid impact to explain dinosaur extinction.

1975
Debate over warm-bloodedness, led by Robert Bakker, begins.

1957
Structure of dinosaur bones gives the first indication that they may have been warm-blooded.

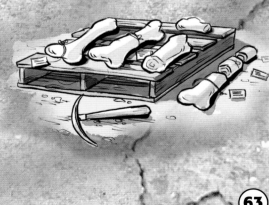

DINOSAUR **DIET**

What does "warm-blooded" mean?

A warm-blooded animal, like a dog or another mammal, generates its own body heat from its food. A cold-blooded animal, like a lizard or another reptile, relies on the temperature of its surroundings for its body heat.

Do they have different lifestyles?

A warm-blooded animal needs more energy than a cold-blooded one. It eats around ten times as much food.

So, were dinosaurs warm-blooded or cold-blooded?

The active meat-eating theropods would have been at the warm-blooded end of the scale, and the big plant-eating sauropods toward the cold-blooded end.

Were there fish-eating dinosaurs?

Yes. Baryonyx and Suchomimus both had a long claw on the thumb—great for hooking fish out of a river. Also, the one good skeleton of Baryonyx found had fish scales in its stomach.

Were dinosaurs exclusively meat eaters or plant eaters?

Some, such as Ornithomimus, were part of the meat-eating theropod group, but they probably ate plants as well.

Did plant eaters eat grass?

Since grass did not really appear until after the dinosaurs had died out, we used to think that no dinosaur ate grass. However, in the early 2000s, a sauropod fossil was found with the remains of primitive grass in its stomach.

FOSSILS

Why are dinosaur footprints more common than skeleton fossils?

Because during its life every animal will leave millions of footprints, but only one skeleton, and it leaves that when it dies.

How can we see inside a dinosaur egg?

A fossilized dinosaur egg is a solid lump of stone. We cannot break it open without destroying it. Scientists sometimes use CAT-scanning facilities from hospitals to see what is inside fossils.

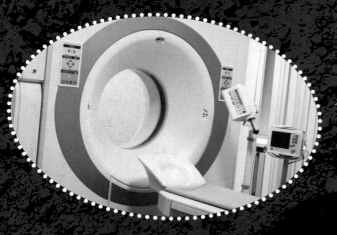

Why are there so few marks left by tails?

We used to think that sauropods lived in water and that the tails floated. Now it seems that the tails were held off the ground by using tendons and muscles.

What is a trace fossil?

It is a fossil of the marks left by an animal—footprints, skin impressions, eggs—rather than of the animal itself.

Do fossils show what a dinosaur ate?

A cololite is a fossil of an animal's meal, still in its stomach. The skeleton of the ankylosaur *Minmi* from Australia contained a cololite—a rare find for a herbivore. The animal had been eating ferns and primitive flowers just before it died.

How do we study dinosaur footprints that are found halfway up a cliff?

Scientists have to climb up to them, but there is a risk that they will either damage themselves or the footprints. An alternative is to use radar scanning. A series of delicate dinosaur footprints on a steep surface in Spain were recently scanned using radar.

Footprints are pressed into the ground, so why do many dinosaur footprints stick out of the rock?

A dinosaur leaves a footprint as a depression. This depression can later be filled by sediment.

This infilling sediment forms a three-dimensional cast of the original, and this is what is often found as a fossil.

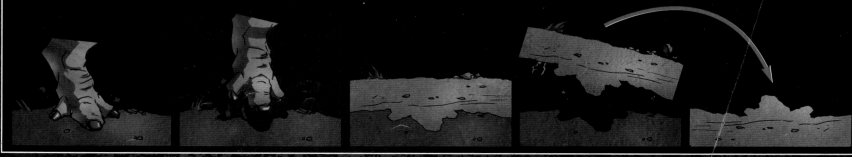

VELOCIRAPTOR

What type of dinosaur was *Velociraptor*?

Velociraptor and its relatives (sometimes called "raptors" or, more scientifically accurate, "dromaeosaurids") were a group of small, meat-eating theropods. They all had a killing claw on the second toe of the hind foot.

Velociraptor was around 7 ft. (2 m) long

How flexible were *Velociraptor's* hands?

Hold your hand up and bring the tips of all the fingers and the thumb together. *Velociraptor* could do this with its three fingers!

Did they hunt in packs?

In 2007, Chinese scientists found tracks of several *Velociraptor* that had been walking by a stream. This indicates that they were hunting in packs.

How did the killer claw work?

The second toe had a huge claw that was used for killing. Its joints were like those of a cat's, and it could lift the huge claw out of the way when it was walking.

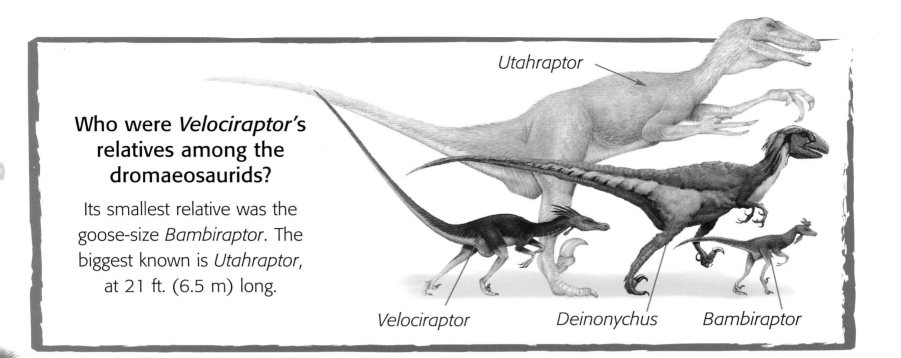

Who were *Velociraptor's* relatives among the dromaeosaurids?

Its smallest relative was the goose-size *Bambiraptor*. The biggest known is *Utahraptor*, at 21 ft. (6.5 m) long.

Utahraptor

Velociraptor   Deinonychus   Bambiraptor

Where did *Velociraptor* live?

Velociraptor lived in Asia. Its relatives have been found in Europe and North America, so we thought that they only existed in the Northern Hemisphere. Then, in 2005, *Neuquenraptor* and *Buitreraptor* turned up in Argentina.

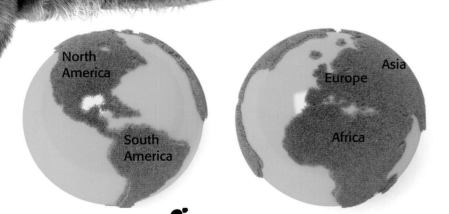

North America

South America

Asia

Europe

Africa

Was the *Velociraptor* in *Jurassic Park* accurate?

No, the movie version was actually based on its close relative *Deinonychus*, which was bigger. One of the scientists who consulted on the movie regarded *Deinonychus* as a species of *Velociraptor*.

WHAT LIVED ALONGSIDE
THE DINOSAURS?

What flew around dinosaurs' heads?

Before birds appeared (around halfway through the age of dinosaurs), pterosaurs were the main flying animals. It appears that dinosaurs ate these flying creatures. A pterosaur bone has been found with a dinosaur tooth embedded in it.

There were also gliding lizards. *Xianlong* was an early Cretaceous lizard, 5 in. (15 cm) long with gliding wings that were formed from its extended ribs.

Were there snakes in the Jurassic?

Maybe. The problem is that snake bones look very similar to lizard bones. Many bones have been found dating from the late Jurassic period, but are they from lizards or snakes?

Was there anything scarier than a dinosaur?

Sarcosuchus, from the early Cretaceous of Africa, was a crocodile 39 ft. (12 m) long. This monster ate dinosaurs!

There were lots of other crocodiles, too. There were long-legged running types and species that evolved to live in the sea.

Were the dinosaurs bothered by pesky insects?

Undoubtedly. There were so many insect types around at the time that some of them must have fed on dinosaur blood.

DINOSAUR DEATH
AND DISEASES

Who was the first person to diagnose a sick dinosaur?

George Baur identified abnormal growth on the bones of the foot of a *Ceratosaurus*. We still do not know the cause of this growth.

Can we tell if dinosaurs were diseased or not?

Most diseases, such as those caused by viruses or parasites, do not leave any trace on the skeleton. Only if the disease affects the bones or the joints can we see any evidence of illness.

Did dinosaurs get toothaches?

There has been only one example of tooth rot among the hundreds of teeth in duck-billed dinosaur jaws. There are sometimes damaged and broken teeth in *Allosaurus* and *Tyrannosaurus* jaws.

Dinosaurs that ate too much red meat sometimes suffered from gout.

Did dinosaurs get cancer?

Odd growths found on particular bones suggest that some dinosaurs may have contracted cancer. However, further study is needed before we can be sure that this was the case.

What was the most common bone damage in dinosaurs?

When an animal is very heavy, the bones of the back tend to fuse to one another, and the animal becomes less flexible. We occasionally see this in fossilized skeletons.

EXTINCTION

How did dinosaurs become extinct?

All types of ideas have been put forward over the years. However, most scientists believe that 65 million years ago, Earth was hit by a giant meteorite, landing in the area of present-day Mexico. The damage caused killed off most of the big animals at the time, including the dinosaurs.

What type of damage occurred?

Immediate damage would have been a shock wave, like that from a nuclear explosion. Then a tsunami would have swept over neighboring lowlands. Red-hot dust in the sky would have acted like a grill and roasted everything beneath it. When the dust had cooled, cloud would have blocked out the Sun so that nothing grew.

Is that the only theory?

Another idea is that volcanic eruptions of the time caused the same type of damage and brought about the extinction. In fact, half of the continent of India is made up of lava flows—some 1 mi. (2 km) thick—that erupted at around that time.

Are there any specific figures?

Within 10,000 years, the carbon dioxide content of the atmosphere quadrupled. The average temperature went up by 45.5°F (7.5°C).

What else became extinct?

This table shows the percentage of things that died out.

Fish	15
Birds	75
Marsupial mammals	75
Placental mammals	14
Amphibians	0
Turtles	27
Lizards	6
Crocodiles	36
Dinosaurs	100
Pterosaurs	100
Plesiosaurs	100
Ichthyosaurs	100

What died first?

Calculations show that the meteorite came from the southeast at an angle of 20 to 30 degrees. The explosion would have sent debris over North America, killing everything there first. A tsunami caused by the impact swept 186 mi. (300 km) inland across southern North America. The rest of the world was then affected by the cloud of dust that spread out from there.

Did all the dinosaurs die out on the same day?

It may have taken tens of thousands of years for the effects to have been fully felt—a very short interval on the geological timescale.

What would have happened if the dinosaurs had not become extinct?

You would not be here reading this book. It is only because the dinosaurs died out that the mammals, including ourselves, were able to take their place and evolve into the fauna that we know today.

DO DINOSAURS
LIVE TODAY?

Birds are directly descended from the meat-eating dinosaurs. Some scientists actually classify birds as dinosaurs. They use the term "nonavian dinosaurs" for conventional dinosaurs.

What birdlike features did dinosaurs have?

The turkey-size *Velociraptor*, also a dromaeosaurid, had a joint in the wrist that enabled the hand to be folded back along the forearm. This is exactly how a bird folds its wings.

An almost complete skeleton of a *Bambiraptor* was found in the late 1990s. It was the smallest of the dromaeosaurids and, just like a bird, was warm-blooded and covered in feathers. Its bones and joints were all birdlike, too.

Velociraptor

Bambiraptor

Hoatzin

Archaeopteryx

What was the first bird?

Archaeopteryx, from the late Jurassic, is the earliest bird known. It had wings of flying feathers, exactly like those of today's birds, but also had many dinosaur-like features: toothy jaws instead of a beak, clawed fingers on the wings, and a long, bony tail.

Do any modern birds have claws on their wings?

The hoatzin of South America has claws on its wings as a chick. The claws help the birds clamber around in trees, but they lose them when they are older.

Is there chemical evidence that birds evolved from dinosaurs?

Protein extracted from sauropod eggs in Argentina in 2005 closely resembled proteins from chickens.

GLOSSARY

Alvarezsaurid A group of small theropod dinosaurs with stubby arms and a single claw on each hand.

Amateur Someone who works at something without getting paid.

Ankylosaur A group of ornithischian dinosaurs with armored backs.

Armadillo A small, armored mammal from South America and southern North America.

Camouflage A body pattern that blends into the background, allowing the owner to hide.

Cancer A disease caused by the uncontrolled growth of cells in one part of a body.

Carbon dioxide A gas in the atmosphere that is essential for plant life.

Ceratopsian A group of ornithischian dinosaurs with armor and horns on the head.

Chameleon A type of lizard that can change its skin color.

Chimera A dinosaur skeleton that is made up of the remains of more than one type of animal.

Cold-blooded An animal whose internal heat depends on the temperature of its surroundings. Reptiles and probably some dinosaurs are, and were, cold-blooded.

Cololite Fossilized stomach contents.

Computer-generated imagery A technique in which a computer is used to produce lifelike moving pictures.

Conifer A tree that has needle-shaped leaves and carries its seeds in cones.

Continent A large mass of land, as distinct from the ocean.

Coprolite Fossilized animal dung.

Cretaceous period The period of Earth's history between 145.5 million and 65.5 million years ago.

CAT scanning A process that allows doctors to see and obtain pictures of the insides of people's bodies.

Current The movement of water or wind in a particular direction.

Duck-billed, or duckbill A group of ornithopod dinosaurs that possessed ducklike beaks.

Equator The imaginary line around Earth midway between the North and South poles.

Expedition A journey to find something specific.

Flange A ridge or rim that protrudes from something, usually for some mechanical reason.

Fossil The remains of a living thing found preserved in the rocks.

Geologist A scientist who studies the rocks and makeup of Earth.

Glide To travel through the air using outstretched wings as support, as opposed to flying, which involves actually flapping the wings to produce lift.

Gout Inflammation of the joints caused by a very rich diet.

Hatchling A baby animal newly hatched from the egg.

Herbivore An animal that eats plants.

Horn A tough, flexible substance made from keratin, the same material as your fingernails. Structures that we call horns usually consist of a bony core covered with keratin.

Jurassic period The period of Earth's history between 199.6 million and 145.5 million years ago.

Lava flow Rock that flows out of a volcano.

Mace A club with a spiked head.

Mesozoic The era of Earth's history that includes the Triassic, Jurassic, and Cretaceous periods.

Metabolism The way a body works.

Museum A building that stores and displays items of interest.

Ornithischian One of the two major groups of dinosaurs, defined by the birdlike arrangement of hip bones.

Ornithopod A group of ornithinischian dinosaurs with birdlike feet.

Oxygen A gas in the atmosphere that is essential for animal life.

Paleontologist A scientists who studies fossils and the past. It is spelled "palaentologist" in other parts of the world.

Pangaea The name given to the supercontinent that existed in the Triassic period.

Panthalassa The name given to the huge ocean that covered the the globe during the time of the supercontinent Pangaea.

Parasite An organism that feeds from another without killing it.

Precocial The term given to an animal that is able to support itself as soon as it is born.

Professional Someone with a career or occupation that earns them money.

Prosauropod A group of sasurischian dinosaurs that were primitive versions of the long-necked sauropods.

Pterosaur A group of flying reptiles from the Mesozoic that were closely related to dinosaurs but were not actually dinosaurs.

Saurischian One of the two major groups of dinosaurs, defined by the lizardlike arrangement of hip bones.

Sauropod A group of saurischian dinosaurs consisting of the long-necked plant eaters.

Stegosaur A group of ornithischian dinosaurs with plates and spines on the back.

Supercontinent All the continents of the world joined together to make a giant landmass.

Swiss Army Knife A folding knife with all types of tools and blades.

Tectonic plate A large panel of Earth's surface that is continually growing from one edge and being destroyed at the other. This means that the surface of Earth is constantly moving and any continent embedded in such a plate is moved around, producing continental drift.

Tendon A tough, flexible strap of gristly substance that connects the bones to one another.

Theropod A group of saurischian dinosaurs. All meat eaters were theropods.

Thyreophoran A group of ornithischian dinosaurs that comprises the stegosaurs and the ankylosaurs.

Triassic period The period of Earth's history between 251 million and 199.6 million years ago.

Tsunami A giant sea wave, usually caused by an earthquake.

Vertebrae The bones of the backbone.

Virus A simple living thing consisting of little more than a molecule that can reproduce itself.

Volcano A vent through which molten material from inside Earth escapes to the surface.

Warm-blooded An animal whose metabolism is such that it can generate its own internal heat. A warm-blooded animal is more active than a cold-blooded one. Mammals, birds, and probably some dinosaurs are, and were, warm-blooded.

INDEX